THE MILLIONAIRE
MINDSET

Unlocking 10 Proven Strategies for
Limitless Wealth

Henry E. Shaffer

Henry E. Shaffer

Acknowledgments:

Writing a book is never a solitary endeavor, and "The Millionaire Mindset" is no exception. It is with immense gratitude and appreciation that I acknowledge the individuals and support systems that have contributed to the creation of this book.

First and foremost, I would like to express my deepest gratitude to the readers and aspiring individuals who have embarked on the journey of cultivating a millionaire mindset. Your curiosity, commitment, and desire for growth have inspired me to create this comprehensive guide, and I am honored to be a part of your transformational journey.

I extend my heartfelt appreciation to my family and friends who have provided unwavering support and encouragement throughout the writing process. Your belief in me and your constant reminders of the importance of sharing knowledge and empowering others have been instrumental in bringing this book to life.

I extend my gratitude to the countless authors, thought leaders, and experts whose work has influenced and shaped my understanding of wealth creation, personal growth, and mindset transformation. Your wisdom and insights have served as a guiding light in the creation of this book.

I would also like to acknowledge the diligent efforts of the editors, proofreaders, and publishing professionals who have worked tirelessly to refine and polish this manuscript. Your keen eye for detail and commitment to excellence have contributed to the overall quality of the final product.

Lastly, I want to express my deep appreciation to the readers who have provided valuable feedback, suggestions, and encouragement. Your engagement and enthusiasm have fueled my passion for empowering individuals to unlock their full potential and achieve financial abundance.

To all those who have played a part, big or small, in the creation of "The Millionaire Mindset," please accept my heartfelt thanks. Your support, encouragement, and contributions have been invaluable, and I am grateful for the opportunity to share this journey with each and every one of you.

May this book serve as a catalyst for transformation, inspiration, and empowerment as you embrace the millionaire mindset and create a life of abundance, purpose, and fulfillment.

With deep appreciation,

[Henry E. Shaffer]

About the Author

Henry E. Shaffer is a renowned entrepreneur, investor, and advocate for the millionaire mindset. With decades of experience in the world of finance and wealth management, he has dedicated his career to empowering individuals to achieve financial independence and create extraordinary wealth.

Born and raised in a modest background, Henry's journey to success is a testament to the transformative power of adopting a millionaire mindset. He understood from an early age that financial abundance was not solely determined by external circumstances but by the mindset, beliefs, and actions one takes towards wealth creation.

Driven by a deep desire to share his knowledge and help others unlock their financial potential, Henry embarked on a mission to study and learn from the most successful individuals in the world of finance. He immersed himself in a wide range of disciplines, including personal development, psychology, investment strategies, and entrepreneurship.

Through his extensive research and personal experiences, Henry developed a unique approach to wealth creation that encompasses not only financial success but also personal growth, purpose, and making a positive impact on society. He believes that true wealth is not solely measured by monetary gains but by the ability to live a fulfilling life, make a difference in the lives of others, and leave a lasting legacy.

Henry's expertise and insights have been sought after by individuals from all walks of life, ranging from aspiring entrepreneurs to seasoned investors. He has conducted workshops, seminars, and mentoring programs, empowering countless individuals to shift their mindset, take control of their finances, and create a roadmap to financial independence.

As an author, Henry E. Shaffer is dedicated to sharing his knowledge and experiences with a wider audience. His writing combines practical strategies, mindset shifts, and inspiring stories to provide a comprehensive guide for those who aspire to achieve financial abundance and unlock their full potential.

Henry's passion for empowering individuals to cultivate a millionaire mindset goes beyond the pages of his books. He actively engages with his readers, providing guidance, support, and inspiration through various platforms, including social media, podcasts, and speaking engagements.

When he is not immersed in the world of finance and personal development, Henry enjoys spending time with his family, pursuing his hobbies, and giving back to the community through philanthropic endeavors. He believes that true wealth is not only about what one accumulates but about the positive impact one creates in the lives of others.

Henry E. Shaffer's mission is to empower individuals to break free from limiting beliefs, embrace the millionaire mindset, and create a life of abundance, purpose, and fulfillment. Through his work, he continues to inspire and guide individuals on their journey to financial independence and extraordinary success.

Connect with Henry E. Shaffer on social media, visit his website, and join him on the path to unlocking your full financial potential and embracing the millionaire mindset.

Introduction:

Embracing the Millionaire Mindset

Meet Henry E. Shaffer, a man who defied all odds and transformed his life from one of financial struggle to incredible abundance. Henry's story is a testament to the power of adopting a millionaire mindset—a mindset that transcends circumstances, dismantles limiting beliefs, and paves the way for extraordinary wealth creation.

Growing up in a modest neighborhood, Henry was no stranger to the hardships that often accompany a lack of financial resources. He witnessed his parents working tirelessly to make ends meet, living paycheck to paycheck with little hope for a brighter future. As a young child, he internalized these struggles and resigned himself to a life of mediocrity.

However, fate had a different plan for Henry. One fortuitous day, he crossed paths with a successful entrepreneur who took notice of his determination and hunger for knowledge. Recognizing the spark of potential within Henry, the entrepreneur gifted him a book that would forever change the trajectory of his life: "The Millionaire Mindset."

But one fateful day, everything changed for Henry. He stumbled upon a worn-out book in a dusty corner of a local library, titled "The Millionaire Mindset." Intrigued by the promise of unlocking the secrets to wealth creation, he eagerly delved into its pages.

As he immersed himself in the book, Henry discovered that becoming a millionaire wasn't solely about luck or innate talent. It was about adopting a unique mindset, a way of thinking that differentiated the wealthy from the rest. The book revealed ten powerful principles that had been time-tested by successful individuals throughout history.

Driven by curiosity and a burning desire to change his circumstances, Henry devoted himself to understanding and applying these principles. With unwavering determination, he embarked on a journey that would reshape his beliefs, actions, and ultimately, his financial destiny.

Through relentless perseverance, Henry transformed himself from a person trapped in the limitations of scarcity to someone who embraced the possibilities of abundance. He applied the principles he learned, embracing the habits and strategies that were instrumental in propelling him towards incredible wealth.

As Henry delved into the pages of this invaluable tome, he discovered a world of possibilities he had never imagined. The book illuminated the fact that wealth creation was not exclusive to a select few; it was a mindset, a set of beliefs, habits, and strategies that anyone could adopt.

In awe and curiosity, Henry immersed himself in the stories of self-made millionaires and their philosophies. He learned that financial success was not simply the result of luck or chance, but rather a deliberate and intentional way of thinking. These individuals possessed a unique perspective on wealth—one that enabled them to spot opportunities, overcome challenges, and build a life of abundance.

Inspired by the stories and wisdom contained within the book, Henry embarked on a personal quest to transform his mindset and reshape his financial reality. He devoured knowledge, sought out mentors, and implemented the principles he had learned. Day by day, his thinking shifted, and with it, his actions and results.

Through persistence, perseverance, and a burning desire for a better life, Henry began to witness remarkable changes unfold. His income multiplied, investments flourished, and doors of opportunity swung open. What was once a distant dream had become his lived reality.

Now, Henry's journey serves as an inspiration and a blueprint for others who yearn for financial freedom and abundance. In this book, "The Millionaire Mindset," we dive deep into the ten fundamental principles that guided Henry towards his financial breakthrough. It is a roadmap that will empower you to cultivate the same mindset, enabling you to attract wealth, manifest opportunities, and create a life of profound prosperity.

Throughout these pages, we will explore the power of belief, the importance of goal-setting, and the strategies for effective money management. We will uncover the secrets of successful investing, entrepreneurial prowess, and the art of creating multiple streams of income. Each chapter will unlock a key element of the millionaire mindset, equipping you with the tools and knowledge necessary to unleash your wealth potential.

Are you ready to embark on this transformative journey? The path to financial abundance and unparalleled success lies before you. Prepare to challenge your existing beliefs, transcend limitations, and embrace the mindset of a millionaire. The time has come to claim your rightful place among those who have mastered the art of wealth creation. Let's begin our exploration of the ten profound principles that will unlock your millionaire mindset and shape your destiny.

Chapter 1:

Rewiring Your Money Mindset: Building a Foundation for Financial Success

Introduction:

Your journey to wealth and abundance begins with a single step—a step that takes you deep into the realm of your own mind. In this pivotal chapter, we will explore the crucial importance of rewiring your money mindset. By understanding and reshaping your beliefs about money, you lay the foundation for a prosperous and fulfilling life.

1.1 The Power of Belief:

Beliefs are the lenses through which we perceive and interpret the world. They shape our thoughts, emotions, and actions, ultimately determining our financial outcomes. In this section, we will uncover the immense power beliefs hold over our lives. We'll explore the impact of both empowering and limiting money beliefs and delve into techniques for identifying and transforming negative beliefs into positive ones.

Through introspection and self-awareness, you will gain clarity on the beliefs that have been holding you back from achieving financial success. Whether it's the belief that money is scarce, that you're not deserving of wealth, or that rich people are inherently greedy, we will work together to challenge and reframe these limiting beliefs. By replacing them with empowering beliefs such as "I am capable of creating wealth" and "Money flows to me easily and abundantly," you will open yourself up to a new realm of possibilities.

1.2 Embracing an Abundance Mentality:

Scarcity mindset breeds fear, anxiety, and a sense of lack. It narrows our vision and keeps us trapped in a cycle of limitation. In contrast, an abundance mentality expands our possibilities and allows us to attract wealth effortlessly. In this part, we'll learn how to shift from a scarcity-driven mindset to one that aligns with the infinite abundance of the universe.

We'll explore gratitude practices that shift your focus from what is lacking to what you already have, cultivating a sense of appreciation for the present moment. Visualization techniques will help you create vivid mental images of your desired financial reality, allowing you to tap into the powerful forces of manifestation. By embracing an abundance mentality, you will attract opportunities, resources, and financial abundance into your life.

1.3 Defining Your Financial Vision:

To manifest wealth, you must first have a clear vision of what financial success means to you. In this section, we'll guide you through the process of defining your financial vision—a compelling and inspiring picture of your desired future.

We'll explore how to set meaningful goals that align with your values and ignite your passion.

By clearly defining your financial vision, you activate the law of attraction and set in motion the forces that will guide you towards your desired outcomes. We'll delve into the process of setting SMART goals—specific, measurable, achievable, relevant, and time-bound—and explore strategies for breaking them down into actionable steps. With a well-defined vision and concrete goals, you'll have a roadmap to navigate your journey to financial freedom.

1.4 Unleashing the Power of Affirmations and Visualization:

Your thoughts have the power to shape your reality. Affirmations and visualization are powerful tools that can reprogram your subconscious mind for success. In this part, we'll uncover the secrets of crafting effective affirmations and creating vivid mental images that align with your financial goals.

Affirmations are positive statements that reinforce your desired beliefs and outcomes. By consistently affirming statements such as "I am abundant in all areas of my life" and "I attract wealth and prosperity effortlessly," you program your subconscious mind to align with these beliefs. Visualization, on the other hand, involves creating detailed mental pictures of your desired financial reality. By regularly visualizing yourself living in abundance, enjoying financial freedom, and achieving your goals, you activate the creative forces of the universe.

We'll provide practical exercises and techniques to integrate affirmations and visualization into your daily life, allowing you to harness their transformative power to reshape your money mindset and attract the wealth you desire.

1.5 Cultivating a Growth Mindset:

Successful individuals understand that failure is not the end but a stepping stone to success. In this section, we'll explore the concept of a growth mindset and how it contributes to financial prosperity. A growth mindset is characterized by a belief that abilities and intelligence can be developed through dedication and hard work.

We'll delve into strategies for embracing challenges, persisting in the face of setbacks, and cultivating resilience and perseverance on your journey to wealth. By adopting a growth mindset, you'll see failures as opportunities for growth, setbacks as temporary obstacles, and effort as the key to mastery. This mindset shift will empower you to take calculated risks, embrace continuous learning, and persistently pursue your financial goals.

1.6 Surrounding Yourself with Success:

Your environment plays a pivotal role in shaping your mindset and influencing your financial outcomes. In this part, we'll discuss the importance of surrounding yourself with individuals who support and uplift your financial aspirations. We'll explore strategies for creating a network of mentors, like-minded peers, and experts who can provide guidance, inspiration, and accountability on your path to financial success.

By immersing yourself in an environment of success and surrounding yourself with individuals who have achieved financial abundance, you'll absorb their mindset, beliefs, and strategies. You'll gain insights, learn from their experiences, and be motivated by their success stories. Together, you'll form a community that fuels your drive for excellence and supports your journey towards the millionaire mindset.

Conclusion:
In this transformative chapter, you have discovered the critical importance of rewiring your money mindset. By acknowledging the

power of your beliefs, embracing abundance, defining your financial vision, harnessing affirmations and visualization, cultivating a growth mindset, and curating a supportive environment, you have laid the groundwork for your journey towards the millionaire mindset.

Remember, your thoughts and beliefs shape your reality. By consciously adopting the mindset of a millionaire, you unlock the door to wealth, abundance, and extraordinary financial success. Get ready to take the next step as we delve into the practical strategies for achieving and sustaining financial prosperity in Chapter 2.

Chapter 2:

Mastering Wealth Creation Strategies: Taking Action for Financial Success

Introduction:

Now that you have laid the foundation of a millionaire mindset in Chapter 1, it's time to dive into the practical strategies that will accelerate your journey to financial success. In this chapter, we will explore the key actions and wealth creation techniques employed by those who have achieved extraordinary abundance. By implementing these strategies, you will propel yourself closer to your financial goals and unlock the doors to wealth and prosperity.

2.1 Building Multiple Streams of Income:

One of the fundamental principles of wealth creation is the concept of diversifying your income sources. In this section, we'll delve into the various ways you can build multiple streams of income. We'll explore strategies such as starting a side business, investing in income-generating assets, and leveraging the power of passive income. By generating income from multiple sources, you create stability, increase your earning potential, and accelerate your wealth-building journey.

We'll guide you through the process of identifying income opportunities, assessing their viability, and creating a plan to implement them effectively. Whether it's through entrepreneurship, real estate, investments, or other avenues, you'll gain insights into how to strategically build and manage multiple streams of income.

2.2 The Art of Strategic Saving and Budgeting:

Financial success is not just about earning money—it's also about effectively managing and growing it. In this part, we'll explore the art of strategic saving and budgeting. We'll provide practical techniques for creating a budget that aligns with your financial goals and helps you allocate your resources efficiently.

You'll learn how to prioritize your spending, eliminate unnecessary expenses, and make informed financial decisions. We'll discuss strategies for saving and investing a portion of your income, allowing your money to work for you and grow over time. By mastering the art of strategic saving and budgeting, you'll gain control over your finances and create a solid foundation for future wealth creation.

2.3 The Secrets of Successful Investing:

Investing is a powerful wealth-building tool employed by millionaires around the world. In this section, we'll unlock the secrets of successful investing. We'll explore different investment vehicles, such as stocks, bonds, real estate, mutual funds, and more. You'll gain insights into how to conduct thorough research, assess risk, and make informed investment decisions.

We'll discuss the importance of diversification, long-term investing strategies, and the power of compounding returns. Whether you're a seasoned investor or just starting, this section will provide you with valuable knowledge and practical tips to navigate the world of investing and maximize your wealth creation potential.

2.4 Leveraging the Power of Entrepreneurship:

Entrepreneurship is a pathway to financial freedom and unlimited potential. In this part, we'll explore the mindset and strategies of successful entrepreneurs. We'll delve into the process of ideation, market analysis, and creating a business plan that sets you up for success.

We'll discuss the importance of finding your passion, identifying a profitable niche, and building a strong brand. You'll learn how to leverage technology, social media, and other resources to scale your business and reach a broader audience. By embracing the entrepreneurial spirit, you'll tap into your creative potential and open doors to immense financial opportunities.

2.5 Developing a Wealth Consciousness:

Wealth is not just about external factors—it starts from within. In this section, we'll explore the importance of developing a wealth consciousness. We'll delve into the mindset shifts necessary to attract and sustain financial abundance.

You'll learn how to overcome limiting beliefs around money, develop a positive relationship with wealth, and cultivate a sense of deservingness. We'll discuss the power of affirmations, visualization, and gratitude in aligning your consciousness with the frequency of wealth. By developing a wealth consciousness, you'll become a magnet for opportunities, synchronicities, and the resources you need to achieve your financial goals.

Conclusion:

In this action-packed chapter, you have explored the practical strategies employed by individuals with a millionaire mindset. By building multiple streams of income, mastering strategic saving and budgeting, embracing successful investing, leveraging the power of entrepreneurship, and developing a wealth consciousness, you are taking decisive steps towards financial success.

Remember, knowledge without action is merely potential. As you implement these wealth creation strategies, stay committed, adapt to changing circumstances, and continually refine your approach. By combining the right mindset with intentional actions, you will unleash your full potential and move closer to the manifestation of your financial dreams. Get ready to dive into Chapter 3, where we'll explore advanced wealth-building techniques and strategies to accelerate your journey to the millionaire mindset.

Chapter 3:

Advanced Wealth-Building Strategies: Accelerating Your Path to Financial Freedom.

Introduction:

In Chapter 3, we will delve deeper into advanced wealth-building strategies that have been instrumental in the success of individuals with a millionaire mindset. These strategies go beyond the basics covered in previous chapters and offer powerful techniques to expedite your journey towards financial freedom. By implementing these advanced strategies, you will gain a competitive edge and elevate your wealth-building efforts to new heights.

3.1 The Power of Leverage:

Leverage is a concept that enables you to achieve more significant results with the resources you have. In this section, we will explore the various forms of leverage and how you can leverage them to your advantage.

Financial leverage involves using borrowed funds to amplify your investment returns. We'll discuss the benefits and risks of leveraging, the concept of leverage ratios, and the importance of managing leverage responsibly. Additionally, we'll explore other types of leverage, such as intellectual leverage, where you leverage your knowledge, expertise, and skills to create exponential results. Technological leverage involves leveraging advancements in technology to automate processes, streamline operations, and scale your business efficiently. Network leverage focuses on leveraging relationships and strategic partnerships to access new opportunities, resources, and markets.

By understanding and utilizing the power of leverage effectively, you can magnify your efforts and achieve accelerated growth and wealth accumulation.

3.2 Strategic Asset Allocation:

Strategic asset allocation is a crucial component of successful wealth management. In this section, we will dive into the intricacies of strategic asset allocation and portfolio management.

You will learn how to assess your risk tolerance and investment objectives to determine an optimal asset allocation strategy. We'll explore different asset classes, including stocks, bonds, real estate, commodities, and alternative investments, and discuss their unique risk-return profiles. We'll delve into the importance of diversification to mitigate risk and enhance portfolio performance. You'll also gain insights into portfolio rebalancing, risk management techniques, and the significance of staying informed about market trends and economic indicators.

By mastering strategic asset allocation, you can optimize your portfolio's returns, protect against downside risks, and foster long-term wealth growth.

3.3 Building and Scaling a Business Empire:

Entrepreneurship offers unparalleled opportunities for wealth creation, and in this section, we will explore advanced strategies for building and scaling a business empire.

We'll delve into the nuances of business growth and expansion, including entering new markets, developing innovative products or services, and implementing effective marketing and sales strategies. You'll gain insights into building a high-performing team, creating systems and processes for scalability, and leveraging technology and automation to streamline operations. We'll discuss the importance of continuous learning, adaptability, and staying ahead of the competition to maintain your business's competitive edge.

By mastering the art of building and scaling a business empire, you can create significant value, generate substantial profits, and unlock limitless potential for wealth creation.

3.4 The Mindset of Abundance and Contribution:

True wealth encompasses more than just financial prosperity—it involves a mindset of abundance and contribution. In this section, we will explore how adopting a mindset of giving and adding value to others can further enhance your financial success.

You'll discover the power of philanthropy and how giving back to society can not only make a positive impact but also attract more abundance into your life. Mentorship will be highlighted as a way to contribute your knowledge and expertise to uplift others while fostering meaningful relationships. We'll discuss the concept of conscious capitalism, where businesses prioritize social and environmental impact, and how this approach can lead to sustainable success.

By aligning your wealth-building endeavors with a higher purpose and incorporating acts of contribution, you'll experience a deeper sense of fulfillment and create a positive ripple effect in the world.

Conclusion:

In this chapter, you have explored advanced wealth-building strategies that can accelerate your path to financial freedom. By leveraging your resources effectively, strategically allocating your assets, building and scaling a business empire, and embracing a mindset of abundance and contribution, you are equipped with the tools to achieve remarkable levels of success.

Remember, these advanced strategies require continuous learning, adaptability, and a commitment to personal growth. As you integrate these techniques into your financial journey, remain focused, be willing to take calculated risks, and stay resilient in the face of challenges. With the millionaire mindset guiding your actions, you are on a path to achieving the wealth, freedom, and abundance you desire.

Get ready for Chapter 4, where we'll explore the principles of wealth preservation, legacy planning, and living a life of true prosperity.

Chapter 4:

Wealth Preservation, Legacy Planning, and Living a Life of True Prosperity

Introduction:

In Chapter 4, we will delve into the crucial aspects of wealth preservation, legacy planning, and the pursuit of true prosperity. Building a fortune is just the beginning; it's equally important to protect and grow that wealth, leaving a lasting legacy for future generations. By understanding the principles and strategies outlined in this chapter, you will not only safeguard your financial achievements but also experience a sense of fulfillment and abundance that transcends monetary wealth.

4.1 The Importance of Wealth Preservation:

Wealth preservation is the foundation of long-term financial security and success. In this section, we will explore the significance of protecting and preserving your wealth. We'll discuss the potential risks and pitfalls that can erode your wealth if not managed effectively.

You'll learn about the importance of diversification, asset protection strategies, and risk management techniques. We'll delve into the world of insurance, trusts, and estate planning, providing you with insights into how these tools can safeguard your assets and provide for your loved ones in the future. By understanding the principles of wealth preservation, you can shield your wealth from unforeseen circumstances and create a solid foundation for lasting financial prosperity.

Benefits of Wealth Preservation:

- Ensures the security and stability of your financial assets.
- Protects your wealth from potential risks, such as market volatility, economic downturns, and legal liabilities.

- Provides a safety net for you and your family, ensuring their financial well-being in the event of unforeseen circumstances.
- Preserves your wealth across generations, allowing your family to benefit from your hard work and success.
- Offers peace of mind and reduces stress, knowing that your financial future is secure.

4.2 Legacy Planning: Creating a Lasting Impact:

Legacy planning is about leaving a meaningful and lasting impact beyond financial wealth. In this part, we'll explore the process of crafting your legacy and the benefits it brings to your life and the lives of others.

You'll learn how to define your values, passions, and purpose, and align them with your wealth and influence. We'll discuss the importance of philanthropy and how giving back can bring immense joy and fulfillment. You'll gain insights into creating a legacy plan that encompasses not only financial considerations but also your values, wisdom, and the impact you wish to make on future generations. By incorporating your personal values into your legacy, you can create a lasting impact that goes far beyond monetary wealth.

Benefits of Legacy Planning:

- Provides a sense of purpose and fulfillment by aligning your wealth with your values and leaving a positive impact on society.
- Preserves your family's values and traditions, ensuring they are carried forward for generations to come.
- Inspires and motivates others through your story, wisdom, and experiences.
- Creates a sense of unity and shared purpose within your family and community.

- Leaves a lasting legacy that transcends monetary wealth and brings joy and fulfillment.

4.3 Living a Life of True Prosperity:

True prosperity extends beyond financial wealth—it encompasses holistic well-being and fulfillment in all areas of life. In this section, we'll explore the principles of living a life of true prosperity and the transformative benefits it brings.

We'll delve into the importance of balance and harmony in key areas such as health, relationships, personal growth, and spirituality. You'll discover strategies for cultivating a positive mindset, practicing gratitude, and nurturing self-care. We'll discuss the significance of aligning your actions with your values and living a life of purpose and authenticity. By embracing true prosperity, you can experience a profound sense of joy, fulfillment, and abundance in every aspect of your life.

Benefits of Living a Life of True Prosperity:

- Enhances overall well-being and happiness by prioritizing physical, emotional, and spiritual health.
- Cultivates meaningful relationships and connections with loved ones, fostering a sense of belonging and support.
- Facilitates personal growth and self-discovery, unlocking your full potential.
- Brings a sense of purpose and fulfillment by aligning your actions with your values and passions.
- Creates a state of abundance and gratitude, attracting more positive experiences and opportunities into your life.

Conclusion:

In this comprehensive chapter, you have explored the critical aspects of wealth preservation, legacy planning, and living a life of true prosperity. By implementing the strategies and principles discussed, you can safeguard your wealth, leave a lasting impact, and experience holistic abundance in all areas of your life.

Remember, wealth is not solely measured by monetary assets but by the impact you make, the values you uphold, and the legacy you leave behind. By adopting the millionaire mindset and integrating these practices into your life, you can truly achieve the pinnacle of success and fulfillment.

Now, brace yourself for Chapter 5, where we'll uncover the secrets of cultivating a wealthy mindset and tapping into the unlimited abundance of the universe.

Chapter 5:

Cultivating a Wealthy Mindset: Unlocking Unlimited Abundance

Introduction:

In Chapter 5, we will dive deep into the transformative power of cultivating a wealthy mindset. Your mindset is the foundation of your financial success, as it shapes your beliefs, thoughts, and actions. By adopting a millionaire mindset, you can tap into the unlimited abundance of the universe and manifest extraordinary wealth and prosperity. In this chapter, we will explore the principles, strategies, and practices that will help you cultivate a mindset of wealth and abundance.

5.1 Understanding the Power of Beliefs:

Beliefs are the lenses through which we perceive the world and shape our reality. In this section, we will explore the power of beliefs and their influence on your financial success.

You'll learn how to identify and challenge limiting beliefs that may be holding you back from achieving your full potential. We'll delve into the concept of abundance mindset and how to shift from scarcity thinking to a mindset of unlimited possibilities. We'll discuss the importance of self-belief, resilience, and perseverance in overcoming challenges and setbacks. By understanding and reshaping your beliefs, you can create a fertile ground for wealth and abundance to flourish.

Benefits of Cultivating Empowering Beliefs:

- Opens up a world of possibilities and opportunities for financial success.
- Boosts confidence and self-esteem, empowering you to take bold actions and seize lucrative ventures.

- Fosters resilience and a positive attitude, enabling you to bounce back from setbacks and failures.
- Enhances creativity and problem-solving abilities, leading to innovative wealth-building strategies.
- Attracts like-minded individuals and mentors who can support and guide you on your journey.

5.2 Harnessing the Power of Visualization and Affirmations:

Visualization and affirmations are powerful tools for reprogramming your subconscious mind and aligning it with your financial goals. In this part, we'll explore the techniques of visualization and affirmations and their impact on your wealth manifestation.

You'll learn how to create vivid mental images of your desired financial outcomes and immerse yourself in the emotions of already having achieved them. We'll discuss the power of affirmations and how to craft empowering statements that reinforce your millionaire mindset. We'll also explore the role of gratitude in amplifying the manifestation process. By consistently practicing visualization, affirmations, and gratitude, you can rewire your subconscious mind for wealth and abundance.

Benefits of Visualization and Affirmations:

- Programs your subconscious mind for success, attracting wealth and abundance into your life.
- Enhances focus and clarity, allowing you to identify and seize lucrative opportunities.
- Strengthens your belief in your ability to achieve your financial goals.
- Boosts motivation and perseverance, fueling your actions towards wealth creation.
- Amplifies the Law of Attraction, magnetizing the resources and circumstances needed for your success.

5.3 Embracing a Growth Mindset:

A growth mindset is essential for continual learning, development, and adaptability on your wealth-building journey. In this section, we'll explore the principles of a growth mindset and its impact on your financial success.

You'll discover the power of embracing challenges, viewing failures as learning opportunities, and persisting in the face of obstacles. We'll discuss the importance of lifelong learning and seeking out mentors who can guide and inspire you. You'll gain insights into the concept of embracing calculated risks and stepping outside of your comfort zone to unlock new levels of wealth and success. By cultivating a growth mindset, you can expand your capabilities, maximize your potential, and achieve extraordinary financial results.

Benefits of Embracing a Growth Mindset:

- Facilitates continuous learning and personal development, keeping you ahead of the curve.
- Enables you to adapt to changing market trends and seize emerging opportunities.
- Enhances problem-solving skills and creative thinking, leading to innovative wealth creation strategies.
- Cultivates resilience and perseverance, enabling you to overcome challenges and setbacks.
- Fosters a sense of fulfillment and joy through the journey of growth and self-improvement.

5.4 Mastering the Law of Attraction:

The Law of Attraction states that like attracts like, and by aligning your thoughts, emotions, and actions with your financial goals, you can manifest wealth and abundance into your life. In this part, we'll explore the principles of the Law of Attraction and its practical application for wealth creation.

You'll learn how to cultivate a positive vibration by focusing on gratitude, joy, and abundance in all areas of your life. We'll discuss the importance of clarity in setting specific financial goals and intentions. You'll gain insights into the role of inspired action and the power of synchronicities and opportunities that arise when you are in alignment with your desires. By mastering the Law of Attraction, you can harness the universal forces to attract the wealth and abundance you desire.

Benefits of Mastering the Law of Attraction:

- Amplifies your ability to attract wealth, resources, and opportunities into your life.
- Enhances your intuition and inner guidance, helping you make aligned and empowered financial decisions.

- Creates a positive and magnetic energy field that draws supportive individuals and circumstances.
- Cultivates a sense of flow and ease in your wealth-building endeavors.
- Aligns your external reality with your internal desires and intentions, leading to profound fulfillment.

Conclusion:

In this expansive chapter, you have explored the principles, strategies, and practices to cultivate a wealthy mindset. By understanding the power of beliefs, harnessing visualization and affirmations, embracing a growth mindset, and mastering the Law of Attraction, you can unlock the unlimited abundance that the universe has to offer.

Remember, cultivating a wealthy mindset is an ongoing process that requires consistency, dedication, and self-awareness. By integrating these practices into your daily life, you will align your thoughts, emotions, and actions with your financial goals, leading to extraordinary wealth and prosperity.

Now, get ready for the final chapter, where we'll wrap up your journey towards embracing the millionaire mindset and outline practical steps to implement all that you have learned into your life for lasting financial success.

Chapter 6:

Implementing the Millionaire Mindset: Practical Steps for Lasting Financial Success

Introduction:

In the final chapter of "The Millionaire Mindset," we will focus on the practical steps you can take to implement the principles and strategies discussed throughout the book. It's time to put your newfound knowledge into action and embark on a path of lasting financial success. By following the guidelines outlined in this chapter, you will lay a strong foundation for wealth creation and develop the habits and routines that will propel you towards your goals.

6.1 Creating a Comprehensive Wealth Plan:

A comprehensive wealth plan serves as a roadmap to guide your financial journey. In this section, we'll explore the essential components of a robust wealth plan and how to create one tailored to your specific goals and circumstances.

You'll learn how to assess your current financial situation, set realistic and measurable goals, and develop strategies to achieve them. We'll discuss the importance of budgeting, saving, and investing wisely to maximize your wealth accumulation. You'll gain insights into the power of compounding and the different asset classes that can generate long-term wealth growth. By creating a comprehensive wealth plan, you can set yourself up for financial success and track your progress along the way.

Benefits of Creating a Comprehensive Wealth Plan:

- Provides clarity and direction in your financial journey.
- Helps you set specific and achievable financial goals.
- Enables you to make informed decisions about budgeting, saving, and investing.

- Allows you to track your progress and make adjustments as needed.
- Instills discipline and accountability in managing your finances.

6.2 Building Multiple Streams of Income:

Relying on a single income source can limit your financial growth and security. In this part, we'll explore the concept of building multiple streams of income and its significance in creating lasting wealth.

You'll learn about different types of income streams, such as active income (e.g., salary, self-employment) and passive income (e.g., rental income, dividends). We'll discuss strategies for diversifying your income, including starting a side business, investing in real estate, and creating digital products or services. You'll gain insights into the benefits of generating passive income and how it can provide financial freedom and stability. By building multiple streams of income, you can accelerate your wealth accumulation and create a resilient financial foundation.

Benefits of Building Multiple Streams of Income:

- Increases your earning potential and financial security.
- Provides a buffer against economic downturns or job loss.
- Offers opportunities for wealth acceleration and faster progress towards your financial goals.
- Allows for more flexibility and freedom in how you allocate your time and resources.
- Creates a sense of empowerment and control over your financial destiny.

6.3 Nurturing a Supportive Wealth Network:

Surrounding yourself with a supportive network of like-minded individuals can significantly impact your financial success. In this section, we'll explore the importance of nurturing relationships with mentors, advisors, and peers who can support and guide you on your wealth-building journey.

You'll learn how to identify potential mentors and seek guidance from those who have achieved the level of success you aspire to. We'll discuss the benefits of networking and participating in mastermind groups or financial communities. You'll gain insights into the power of collaboration, knowledge sharing, and leveraging the expertise and connections of others. By nurturing a supportive wealth network, you can gain valuable insights, access new opportunities, and stay motivated and inspired.

Benefits of Nurturing a Supportive Wealth Network:

- Provides guidance, mentorship, and accountability from experienced individuals.

- Offers opportunities for collaboration, joint ventures, and shared resources.
- Expands your knowledge and perspective through exposure to different ideas and strategies.
- Provides a sense of community and support on your wealth-building journey.
- Facilitates personal and professional growth through connections and learning opportunities.

6.4 Embracing a Wealth-Mindful Lifestyle:

To sustain lasting financial success, it's essential to adopt a wealth-mindful lifestyle that aligns with your values and goals. In this part, we'll explore the habits, mindset shifts, and daily practices that can support your journey towards wealth creation.

You'll learn about the importance of mindful spending, making conscious choices about how you allocate your financial resources. We'll discuss the significance of financial literacy and continuous learning to stay informed and make informed financial decisions. You'll gain insights into the benefits of self-care, stress management, and maintaining a healthy work-life balance to ensure long-term well-being on your wealth-building journey. By embracing a wealth-mindful lifestyle, you can cultivate habits that support your financial goals and create a sustainable and fulfilling life.

Benefits of Embracing a Wealth-Mindful Lifestyle:

Promotes mindful and intentional spending, avoiding unnecessary debt and overspending.
Enhances financial literacy and empowers you to make informed decisions.
Supports overall well-being by prioritizing self-care and stress management.
Fosters a healthy work-life balance, avoiding burnout and maintaining long-term productivity.
Creates a sense of alignment and congruence between your financial goals and your daily actions.

Conclusion:

In this final chapter, you have learned the practical steps to implement the millionaire mindset and create lasting financial success. By creating a comprehensive wealth plan, building multiple streams of income, nurturing a supportive wealth network, and embracing a wealth-mindful lifestyle, you can create a solid foundation for wealth creation and live a fulfilling and abundant life.

Remember, the millionaire mindset is not a destination but a lifelong journey of growth, learning, and refinement. Stay committed to your financial goals, remain adaptable to changing circumstances, and continue to cultivate a mindset of abundance and possibility.

As you move forward, embrace the power within you to create the financial future you desire. By integrating the principles and practices discussed in this book into your life, you are well on your way to achieving extraordinary financial success.

Congratulations on embarking on this transformative journey. May you embody the millionaire mindset and unlock the boundless abundance that awaits you.

Chapter 7:

Sustaining and Expanding Your Millionaire Mindset: Thriving in the Realm of Wealth

Introduction:

In the final chapter of "The Millionaire Mindset," we will delve into the critical aspects of sustaining and expanding your millionaire mindset. Building wealth is not a one-time achievement but an ongoing journey that requires continuous growth, adaptation, and expansion. In this chapter, we will explore strategies, habits, and practices that will help you thrive in the realm of wealth and create a lasting legacy of abundance.

7.1 Embracing Lifelong Learning and Growth:

To sustain your millionaire mindset, it's essential to embrace lifelong learning and personal growth. In this section, we'll discuss the importance of expanding your knowledge, acquiring new skills, and staying ahead of the curve in an ever-evolving financial landscape.

You'll learn the benefits of investing in your education, whether through formal education, workshops, seminars, or self-study. We'll explore the power of reading and how it can broaden your perspective, spark creativity, and expose you to new ideas and strategies. Additionally, we'll discuss the significance of staying informed about market trends, emerging technologies, and investment opportunities. By embracing lifelong learning and growth, you can continuously adapt to changes, make informed decisions, and stay at the forefront of wealth creation.

Benefits of Embracing Lifelong Learning and Growth:
- Expands your knowledge and expertise in wealth creation strategies.

- Enhances your problem-solving abilities and adaptability to changing market conditions.
- Sparks creativity and innovation in your wealth-building endeavors.
- Enables you to identify emerging trends and capitalize on new opportunities.
- Fosters personal growth and fulfillment as you continually develop your skills and abilities.

7.2 Cultivating a Mindset of Gratitude and Abundance:

Gratitude and abundance are fundamental pillars of the millionaire mindset. In this part, we'll explore the transformative power of gratitude and how it can expand your wealth consciousness.

You'll learn how to cultivate a daily gratitude practice, acknowledging and appreciating the abundance that already exists in your life. We'll discuss the benefits of shifting your focus from scarcity to abundance, recognizing the infinite possibilities available to you. Additionally, we'll explore the practice of giving back and contributing to causes that align with your values. By cultivating a mindset of gratitude and abundance, you can attract more wealth, joy, and fulfillment into your life.

Benefits of Cultivating a Mindset of Gratitude and Abundance:

- Increases your overall sense of well-being, contentment, and happiness.
- Amplifies your ability to attract and manifest wealth into your life.
- Strengthens your relationships and fosters a sense of connection and generosity.
- Cultivates a positive and optimistic outlook, even in the face of challenges.
- Deepens your appreciation for the journey and the impact you can make in the world.

7.3 Mastering the Art of Wealth Preservation:

Preserving and protecting your wealth is as crucial as creating it. In this section, we'll explore the strategies and principles of wealth preservation, ensuring your financial success endures for future generations.

You'll learn about asset protection strategies, including estate planning, trusts, and legal structures that safeguard your wealth. We'll discuss the importance of diversification and risk management in maintaining a robust financial portfolio. Additionally, we'll explore the role of insurance in mitigating potential risks and liabilities. By mastering the art of wealth preservation, you can ensure that your hard-earned wealth is secure and that your legacy continues to thrive.

Benefits of Mastering the Art of Wealth Preservation:

- Provides peace of mind, knowing that your wealth is protected for future generations.
- Minimizes potential risks and liabilities that can threaten your financial success.
- Maintains the integrity and stability of your financial portfolio.
- Allows you to leave a lasting legacy and make a positive impact on future generations.
- Provides a sense of financial security and freedom.

7.4 Embodying Abundance in All Areas of Life:

The millionaire mindset goes beyond financial success—it encompasses a holistic approach to life. In this part, we'll explore how to embody abundance in all areas of your life, including health, relationships, and personal fulfillment.

You'll learn the significance of self-care and prioritizing your physical, mental, and emotional well-being. We'll discuss the importance of cultivating meaningful relationships and surrounding yourself with a supportive network of like-minded individuals. Additionally, we'll explore the value of aligning your life purpose with your wealth creation efforts. By embodying abundance in all areas of life, you can create a truly fulfilling and balanced existence.

Benefits of Embodying Abundance in All Areas of Life:

- Enhances your overall well-being, vitality, and quality of life.
- Cultivates deep and meaningful connections with loved ones and supportive individuals.
- Provides a sense of fulfillment and purpose beyond financial achievements.
- Creates harmony and balance between your personal and professional life.

- Enables you to live a life of abundance and impact in all areas.

Conclusion:

Congratulations! You have reached the end of "The Millionaire Mindset," a transformative journey towards creating extraordinary wealth and abundance. Throughout this book, you have gained insights into the mindset, strategies, and habits of millionaires, unlocking the keys to financial success.

By implementing the practical steps outlined in this chapter, including embracing lifelong learning and growth, cultivating gratitude and abundance, mastering the art of wealth preservation, and embodying abundance in all areas of life, you are primed to thrive in the realm of wealth.

Remember, the millionaire mindset is not a destination but a lifelong commitment to growth, expansion, and contribution. Stay true to your vision, remain disciplined, and continue to evolve and adapt to changing circumstances. Trust in your abilities and the infinite possibilities that lie ahead.

May your journey towards lasting financial success be filled with joy, fulfillment, and profound abundance. Now go forth and create the extraordinary life you deserve.

Chapter 8:

Leaving a Lasting Legacy: Making an Impact Beyond Wealth

Introduction:

In the final chapter of "The Millionaire Mindset," we will explore the concept of leaving a lasting legacy and making an impact that extends beyond financial success. Building wealth is not just about accumulating riches for oneself—it's about creating a positive and transformative influence on the world. In this chapter, we will delve into the strategies, principles, and mindset shifts that will enable you to leave a lasting legacy and make a meaningful impact.

8.1 Discovering Your Life's Purpose:

To leave a lasting legacy, it's crucial to align your wealth-building efforts with your life's purpose. In this section, we'll explore how to discover your life's purpose and infuse it into your financial pursuits.

You'll learn how to reflect on your passions, values, and strengths to identify your unique purpose. We'll discuss the significance of creating a vision that aligns with your purpose and inspires you to take action. Additionally, we'll explore the power of setting meaningful goals that contribute to your life's purpose. By discovering and aligning with your life's purpose, you can infuse your wealth-building journey with passion, meaning, and a sense of fulfillment.

Benefits of Discovering Your Life's Purpose:

- Provides a sense of direction and meaning in your wealth-building endeavors.
- Ignites passion and motivation to pursue your goals.
- Enhances fulfillment and satisfaction by aligning your actions with your purpose.

- Enables you to make a positive impact and contribute to causes that matter to you.
- Inspires others by living an authentic and purpose-driven life.

8.2 Cultivating a Mindset of Abundance and Contribution:

To leave a lasting legacy, it's crucial to cultivate a mindset of abundance and contribution. In this part, we'll explore how to shift your mindset from scarcity to abundance and channel your resources towards making a positive impact.

You'll learn the importance of practicing gratitude, appreciating what you have, and recognizing the abundance that exists in your life. We'll discuss the power of giving back and the various ways you can contribute to causes that resonate with you, whether through philanthropy, volunteering, or mentorship. Additionally, we'll explore the concept of social entrepreneurship and how you can leverage your wealth and influence to address social and environmental challenges. By cultivating a mindset of abundance and contribution, you can create a lasting legacy that transcends financial success.

Benefits of Cultivating a Mindset of Abundance and Contribution:

- Fosters a sense of purpose and fulfillment beyond material wealth.
- Creates a positive ripple effect by inspiring others to give and make a difference.
- Enhances your sense of connectedness and empathy towards others.
- Provides opportunities for personal growth and learning through your contribution efforts.
- Leaves a positive and transformative impact on society and future generations.

8.3 Building a Sustainable and Ethical Business:

If you are an entrepreneur or aspire to start your own business, building a sustainable and ethical enterprise is a powerful way to leave a lasting legacy. In this section, we'll explore the principles and strategies for creating a business that aligns with your values and has a positive impact.

You'll learn about the significance of ethical business practices, including fair treatment of employees, environmental sustainability, and social responsibility. We'll discuss the benefits of incorporating purpose-driven initiatives into your business model and how it can attract customers, employees, and investors who share your values. Additionally, we'll explore the power of innovation and disruptive thinking in creating businesses that address societal challenges. By building a sustainable and ethical business, you can create a legacy that embodies your values and positively impacts the world.

Benefits of Building a Sustainable and Ethical Business:

- Aligns your business with your values and purpose.
- Attracts customers, employees, and investors who resonate with your mission.
- Enhances your brand reputation and builds trust with stakeholders.
- Contributes to positive social and environmental change.
- Creates a long-lasting and influential legacy in the business world.

8.4 Nurturing Relationships and Mentoring Others:

Leaving a lasting legacy is not solely about financial success—it's also about nurturing relationships and empowering others. In this part, we'll explore the importance of fostering meaningful connections and mentoring the next generation of wealth builders.

You'll learn how to cultivate authentic relationships built on trust, respect, and mutual support. We'll discuss the benefits of mentorship and how sharing your knowledge, experiences, and insights can empower others on their wealth-building journey. Additionally, we'll explore the concept of legacy planning and how you can pass down your values, wisdom, and wealth to future generations. By nurturing relationships and mentoring others, you can create a ripple effect of positive change that extends far beyond your lifetime.

Benefits of Nurturing Relationships and Mentoring Others:

- Creates a network of support and collaboration in your personal and professional life.
- Empowers others to achieve their financial goals and fulfill their potential.
- Enables you to leave a lasting impact on future generations.

- Builds a positive reputation and legacy as a leader and mentor.
- Fosters a sense of fulfillment and purpose in supporting others' growth.

Conclusion:

Congratulations! You have reached the end of "The Millionaire Mindset," a transformative journey towards creating extraordinary wealth and leaving a lasting legacy. By implementing the strategies, principles, and mindset shifts outlined in this chapter, you are well on your way to making a meaningful impact that extends far beyond financial success.

Remember, leaving a lasting legacy is a continuous and intentional endeavor. Stay committed to your purpose, cultivate a mindset of abundance and contribution, build sustainable and ethical businesses, and nurture relationships while empowering others. By embodying these principles, you can create a legacy that not only transforms your own life but also positively influences future generations and leaves an indelible mark on the world.

May your journey towards a lasting legacy be filled with fulfillment, joy, and profound impact. Go forth and make your mark on the world with the millionaire mindset.

Chapter 9:

Embracing Continuous Growth and Evolution: Thriving in an Ever-Changing World

Introduction:

In the dynamic landscape of wealth creation, embracing continuous growth and evolution is essential for maintaining a millionaire mindset. In this final chapter of "The Millionaire Mindset," we will explore the strategies, habits, and mindset shifts necessary to thrive in an ever-changing world.

By adapting to new technologies, market trends, and evolving economic landscapes, you can position yourself for sustained success and navigate through challenges with resilience. In this chapter, we will delve into the importance of continuous learning, embracing innovation, and fostering an agile mindset. Let us embark on this journey of growth and exploration to unlock the secrets of thriving in an ever-changing world.

9.1 The Power of Continuous Learning:

Continuous learning is the key to staying relevant and informed in an ever-evolving world. In this section, we will explore the transformative benefits of embracing lifelong learning and the various avenues for expanding your knowledge and skills.

You will discover the significance of being curious and open-minded, allowing yourself to explore new subjects and ideas. We will discuss the benefits of formal education, online courses, workshops, and mentorship in deepening your expertise. Additionally, we will delve into the importance of staying abreast of industry trends and emerging technologies. By embracing continuous learning, you can remain at the forefront of your field, adapt to change, and seize new opportunities.

Benefits of Continuous Learning:

- Expands your knowledge and expertise, enhancing your professional capabilities.
- Increases your adaptability and agility in a rapidly changing world.
- Fosters personal growth and self-improvement, leading to a more fulfilling life.
- Stimulates creativity and innovation, allowing you to discover new solutions.
- Boosts your confidence and credibility, positioning you as a leader in your industry.

9.2 Embracing Innovation and Adaptability:

Innovation and adaptability are vital traits for maintaining a millionaire mindset in an ever-changing world. In this part, we will explore the mindset and strategies needed to embrace innovation and adapt to new circumstances.

We will delve into the importance of cultivating a growth mindset, which allows you to embrace challenges, learn from failures, and seek out new opportunities. You will discover the benefits of fostering a culture of innovation within yourself and your organization. We will also discuss the value of embracing technology and leveraging it to drive your wealth-building endeavors forward. By embracing innovation and adaptability, you can thrive amidst disruption and position yourself for long-term success.

Benefits of Embracing Innovation and Adaptability:

- Positions you as a forward-thinking and agile individual in your industry.
- Unleashes creativity and encourages out-of-the-box thinking.
- Enables you to seize new opportunities and stay ahead of the competition.
- Facilitates problem-solving and overcoming obstacles with ease.

- Enhances your ability to navigate through uncertain times.

9.3 Cultivating Resilience and Overcoming Challenges:

Resilience is a crucial trait for maintaining a millionaire mindset in the face of adversity and challenges. In this section, we will explore the strategies and mindset shifts necessary to cultivate resilience and overcome obstacles.

You will discover the power of reframing challenges as opportunities for growth and learning. We will discuss the importance of cultivating a positive mindset and developing coping mechanisms to navigate through difficult times. Additionally, we will explore the significance of building a support system and seeking guidance from mentors and like-minded individuals. By cultivating resilience, you can bounce back from setbacks, stay focused on your goals, and continue progressing on your wealth-building journey.

Benefits of Cultivating Resilience:

- Enables you to bounce back from setbacks and maintain focus on your goals.
- Builds emotional strength and mental fortitude.
- Provides a sense of empowerment and self-confidence.
- Cultivates a positive mindset and reduces stress.
- Enhances your ability to adapt to change and overcome challenges.

9.4 Thriving in a Changing World:

Thriving in an ever-changing world requires a combination of adaptability, resilience, and strategic thinking. In this final part, we will bring together the principles and strategies discussed throughout the chapter to help you thrive in a changing world.

You will learn how to cultivate a future-oriented mindset, anticipate trends, and stay ahead of the curve. We will discuss the importance of strategic planning, setting clear goals, and aligning your actions with your vision. Additionally, we will explore the value of networking, building strategic partnerships, and leveraging collaboration to create new opportunities. By embracing continuous growth and evolution, you can position yourself as a leader in your field and adapt to the ever-changing landscape of wealth creation.

Benefits of Thriving in a Changing World:

- Positions you as a thought leader and innovator in your industry.
- Creates a competitive edge and opens doors to new opportunities.
- Enhances your ability to navigate through uncertainty with confidence.
- Fosters personal growth and self-actualization.

- Allows you to maintain long-term success and prosperity.

Conclusion:

Congratulations! You have reached the end of "The Millionaire Mindset," a transformative journey towards building extraordinary wealth and embracing continuous growth. By implementing the strategies, mindset shifts, and habits outlined in this chapter, you are well on your way to thriving in an ever-changing world.

Remember, maintaining a millionaire mindset is a lifelong commitment to growth, adaptability, and embracing change. Continuously seek opportunities for learning, innovation, and personal development. Cultivate resilience, stay focused on your goals, and surround yourself with a supportive network of individuals who uplift and inspire you.

May your journey towards a millionaire mindset be filled with abundance, growth, and profound success. Embrace the ever-changing world with confidence, and continue to create a legacy that transcends generations. Now go forth and thrive in the dynamic landscape of wealth creation.

Chapter 10:

Mastering Wealth Management: Securing and Sustaining Your Financial Success

Introduction:

In the final chapter of "The Millionaire Mindset," we will explore the critical aspect of wealth management, which is essential for securing and sustaining your financial success. Building wealth is not only about accumulating riches but also effectively managing and growing your assets to maintain long-term prosperity. In this chapter, we will delve into the strategies, principles, and mindset shifts required to master wealth management and create a solid foundation for lasting financial abundance.

10.1 Setting Financial Goals and Creating a Plan:

To effectively manage your wealth, it is crucial to set clear financial goals and create a comprehensive plan. In this section, we will explore the process of defining your financial objectives, aligning them with your values, and creating a roadmap to achieve them.

You will learn how to establish short-term and long-term financial goals that encompass various aspects of your life, such as investment targets, savings plans, debt management, and retirement planning. We will discuss the significance of creating a budget, tracking your expenses, and optimizing your cash flow. Additionally, we will explore the value of seeking professional advice from financial planners or wealth advisors to tailor a plan that aligns with your unique circumstances. By setting financial goals and creating a solid plan, you can effectively manage your wealth and work towards your desired financial outcomes.

Benefits of Setting Financial Goals and Creating a Plan:
- Provides clarity and direction in your financial journey.

- Enhances financial discipline and responsibility.
- Facilitates decision-making and prioritization of resources.
- Optimizes your ability to achieve financial milestones.
- Builds a solid foundation for sustainable wealth management.

10.2 Building Multiple Streams of Income:

Diversifying your sources of income is a key strategy for mastering wealth management. In this part, we will explore the benefits and methods of building multiple streams of income to create financial stability and security.

You will discover the various options available for generating additional income, such as investments, real estate, entrepreneurship, and passive income streams. We will discuss the importance of conducting thorough research, analyzing risks, and identifying opportunities in different market sectors. Additionally, we will explore the concept of leveraging your skills, talents, and assets to create income-generating ventures. By building multiple streams of income, you can increase your financial resilience, minimize risk, and create opportunities for wealth accumulation.

Benefits of Building Multiple Streams of Income:

- Reduces reliance on a single source of income and diversifies risk.
- Creates opportunities for exponential wealth growth.
- Provides financial security and stability during economic fluctuations.
- Enables you to explore new ventures and expand your wealth-building potential.
- Enhances your ability to weather financial challenges and protect your assets.

10.3 Effective Investment Strategies:
Investing wisely is a fundamental component of successful wealth management. In this section,

we will explore the principles and strategies for making informed investment decisions that align with your financial goals.

You will learn about the different asset classes, such as stocks, bonds, real estate, and alternative investments, and how to evaluate their potential returns and risks. We will discuss the significance of diversification, asset allocation, and risk management in constructing a well-rounded investment portfolio. Additionally, we will explore the value of staying informed about market trends, conducting due diligence, and seeking expert advice to make informed investment choices. By adopting effective investment strategies, you can optimize your returns, mitigate risks, and create long-term wealth.

Benefits of Effective Investment Strategies:

- Maximizes your investment returns and capital appreciation.

- Mitigates risks through diversification and asset allocation.
- Generates passive income and wealth accumulation.
- Provides opportunities for capital preservation and growth.
- Creates a foundation for financial independence and freedom.

10.4 Tax Planning and Estate Management:

Tax planning and estate management are vital aspects of comprehensive wealth management. In this part, we will explore the importance of tax-efficient strategies and estate planning to protect and preserve your wealth.

You will gain insights into the tax implications of different investment vehicles and how to optimize your tax liability through legal and ethical strategies. We will discuss the benefits of estate planning, including the creation of wills, trusts, and other structures to ensure the smooth transfer of wealth to future generations.

Additionally, we will explore the significance of charitable giving and philanthropy as a way to align your wealth with your values and create a positive impact on society. By effectively managing taxes and planning your estate, you can safeguard your wealth, minimize tax burdens, and leave a lasting legacy.

Benefits of Tax Planning and Estate Management:

- Reduces tax liabilities and preserves wealth.
- Ensures the smooth transfer of assets to heirs and beneficiaries.
- Provides financial security for your loved ones.
- Creates opportunities for philanthropy and social impact.
- Minimizes legal complications and maximizes the value of your estate.

Conclusion:

Congratulations! You have reached the end of "The Millionaire Mindset," a transformative journey towards mastering wealth management and securing your financial success. By implementing the strategies, principles, and mindset shifts outlined in this chapter, you are well-equipped to navigate the complexities of wealth management and create a solid foundation for lasting financial abundance.

Remember, effective wealth management is an ongoing process that requires continuous education, strategic planning, and adaptability to changing market conditions. Stay committed to your financial goals, regularly review and adjust your strategies, and seek professional advice when needed. By mastering wealth management, you can enjoy financial freedom, create a legacy of abundance, and live a life of purpose and fulfillment.

May your journey towards mastering wealth management be filled with prosperity, growth, and profound success. Embrace the principles of the millionaire mindset and unlock the full potential of your financial future. Now, go forth and secure your financial success with confidence and determination.

Conclusion:

Embracing Your Journey to a Millionaire Mindset

Congratulations! You have reached the end of "The Millionaire Mindset," a transformative guide that has taken you on a journey of self-discovery, mindset shifts, and practical strategies to create extraordinary wealth and leave a lasting legacy. Throughout this book, you have gained valuable insights into the mindset, habits, and principles that successful individuals embody to achieve financial abundance and make a meaningful impact on the world.

As you reflect on your journey, remember that the millionaire mindset is not just about accumulating vast sums of money. It encompasses a holistic approach to wealth creation, encompassing financial success, personal growth, positive impact, and a sense of purpose. By embracing the principles outlined in this book and adopting them into your daily life, you have set yourself on a path to greatness and limitless possibilities.

Embracing a millionaire mindset requires a commitment to personal growth and continuous learning. It involves challenging your limiting beliefs, stepping out of your comfort zone, and cultivating a mindset of abundance and gratitude. It is a journey that requires perseverance, resilience, and a willingness to adapt to changing circumstances. Remember, success is not achieved overnight but through consistent effort and dedication.

Throughout this book, you have explored various topics essential to the millionaire mindset, from developing a strong work ethic and embracing financial discipline to creating multiple streams of income and nurturing relationships. You have learned the importance of setting clear goals, creating a comprehensive plan, and taking calculated risks. You have discovered the power of mindset, positive affirmations, and visualization in manifesting your desired outcomes. Moreover, you have understood the significance of ethical and sustainable wealth creation, leaving a positive impact on society, and building a legacy that transcends generations.

As you embark on your journey to a millionaire mindset, keep in mind the following key takeaways:

1. **Mindset Matters:** Cultivate a mindset of abundance, gratitude, and resilience. Believe in your ability to achieve greatness and overcome challenges.

2. **Purpose and Passion:** Align your wealth-building endeavors with your values, passions, and purpose. Success is not just about financial gains but also about finding fulfillment and making a positive impact.

3. **Continuous Learning**: Commit to lifelong learning and personal

development. Stay curious, seek new knowledge, and adapt to evolving trends and technologies.

4. **Discipline and Financial Management:** Practice financial discipline, create a comprehensive plan, and manage your wealth effectively. Embrace strategic investment choices and diversify your sources of income.

5. **Relationships and Mentorship:** Surround yourself with like-minded individuals, build strong relationships, and seek guidance from mentors. Support others on their journey to success.

6. **Legacy and Impact:** Create a lasting legacy by contributing to causes you believe in, engaging in philanthropy, and leaving a positive impact on society.

Remember, the journey to a millionaire mindset is unique to each individual. Your path may have its ups and downs, but with determination, resilience, and a commitment to growth, you have the power to transform your life and create a legacy that inspires others.

Now, armed with the knowledge, insights, and tools shared in this book, go forth and embrace your journey to a millionaire mindset. Dream big, take bold actions, and never lose sight of your potential. Your success awaits you as you embody the millionaire mindset and make your mark on the world.